The ABC's

of Successful Managers

(according to Mikey)

ISBN: 978-1-4303-0308-4

Illustrations by Kathryn and Greg Nunley

DEDICATION

To Bill, Bobby, Kenny, Larry, and "Marvelous" Marvin, I think it's this simple.

At least it was with people like you. I thank each one of you for your support,

your dedication and your commitment to being the "Best of the Best."

FOREWORD

For a long time now, I've thought some people have gone out of their way to make things difficult and confusing for me. For example, why is there so much paperwork involved in buying a car? Has anyone ever sat down and read all the fine print, or for that matter any of the print on those contracts the Dealers wants us to sign? Surely not. Why is all that paperwork needed? I want to buy this car. You have this car. How much do you want for this car? Sounds good to me. I'll write you a check. Here are the keys. See ya. Why all the confusing wordsmithed paperwork? It's sure not that confusing at the grocery store. They have what I want. They tell me the price. I give them the money. I take my groceries and leave. Pretty simple. Let's talk about insurance for a moment. Again, who has the time or eyesight to read all that paperwork? I have car insurance. I'm in an accident. I need my car fixed. Fix it. That's why I pay for insurance right? One would think it would be that simple. But is it? Of course not. It's complicated. WHY??? Have you ever asked someone a question and received an answer like "It's complicated?" Well duh. I'm not stupid. If you don't want to tell me, just say so. Don't question my intellect.

Anyway, I do know that there are things in this world that are complicated. Getting the space shuttle to and from orbit comes to mind. Math and foreign languages are also difficult to understand for some of us. Not so much for others though. So apparently confusing and complicated are relative to individuals. I guess I can understand that. I have however, on occasion asked people, who like to impress others with their vast knowledge, to talk to me like I'm four (4).

You see, when you can satisfactorily explain something to a four (4) year old, you've accomplished something. You have taken a subject usually totally "Greek" to them, and made it clear. Made it understandable. Made it believable to someone who only knows black and white, right and wrong, and good and evil. Life is pretty simple to a four (4) year old. We intelligent adults have made life tough. Can you think about some other examples of taking something pretty "cut and dried" and making it confusing and difficult. I'll bet you have plenty of examples also.

I've been in management for twenty-five years. I've seen a lot of programs come and go. There has to be a more simplistic way to get along with people. Not just in the Labor/Management ranks, but in life in general. I've put together some "ABC's of Management", according to me, that may or may not help you with your career or with your life. I wish I had learned to use them earlier in my tenure. It sure would have made the journey easier.

Anyway, please use what you can. Discard anything you feel inappropriate. However, whatever you do with the information in this book or any other book, strive to improve the quality of life of everyone you come in contact with. That's the message. Pretty simple stuff, huh?

A

Attitude-

Your attitude is your strongest motivational tool, whether

in your personal or professional life. Positive as well as

negative attitudes change everything.

Which Manager would you rather work with?

B

Benefit-

Make sure everyone you come in contact with knows the

benefit they bring to the table every day.

C

Communication-

Perhaps the single most neglected trait of today's

managers. Ensure everyone knows the direction

the Team is headed.

Which would you rather have, a gentle reminder
or someone screaming at you?

D

Delegate-

You can't do it all, nor should you. Your job is to ready

everyone for the next level of responsibility. They can't

be prepared if you don't give them the opportunity.

E

Encourage-

Everyone responds to reward more than punishment.

"When you do something wrong, no one remembers.

When you do something right, no one forgets."

Lift up your family and coworkers!

F

Friendly-

Friendly discussions are less stressful than confrontational ones,

and much more beneficial to everyone involved.

G

Gratitude-

We all are encouraged by a pat on the back. Give them freely.

They really are as important to give as to get.

Thank You

Gracias

Merci

H

Honesty-

You will never be successful without it.

"Nuff" said.

I

I-

Lose this word from your vocabulary.

It doesn't belong in a Team environment.

J

Judicious-

Be fair with everyone and look at each

situation on its own merit.

K

Kindness-

Why would anyone want to be treated any differently? Huh?

L

Loyalty-

If you are loyal to your family and co-workers, they will

be loyal to you.

M

Me-

Lose this word when you lose "I".

Not a part of the winning Team concept.

N

Nice-

Wouldn't it be nice if everyone was treated nicely?

O

Objective-

Be impartial and give everyone a fair shake.

Don't allow your personality to

interfere with the decision making process.

P

Professional-

Be professional in all your dealings,

and expect the same in return.

 **Q**

Quality-

Do everything humanly possible to improve the quality of

life of everyone you come in contact with.

Yours will improve exponentially.

R

Respect-

Respect all persons in all aspects of life

regardless of your station or theirs.

S

Sincerity-

Be sincere in all that you do.

Show empathy, show compassion, show sympathy,

and mean it.

T

Trust-

Is there anything more valued?

I think not.

U

Understanding-

Actively demonstrate understanding in all encounters.

Ensure people know you are listening to them.

V

Value-

Let people know that they themselves, as well as their thoughts

and ideas, are valued by you.

W

We-

The only word needed to build a winning team.

Use this term often for obvious reasons.

X

(e)Xample-

Never forget, you set the standard.

People may not always do as you say,

but they will always do as you do.

Y

You-

Never let the focus get on you, it's always we.

The Team. The Team. The Team.

Z

Zealous-

Demonstrate excitement and commitment in all that you do.

Show everyone that you care.

Wow!

www.ingramcontent.com/pod-product-compliance
Lightning Source LLC
Chambersburg PA
CBHW021922170526
45157CB00005B/2149